WIZARDS

CHRIS LEHOTSKÝ

Cavendish
Square
New York

CREATURES OF FANTASY
WIZARDS

BY

CHRIS LEHOTSKY

CAVENDISH SQUARE PUBLISHING · NEW YORK

Published in 2017 by Cavendish Square Publishing, LLC
243 5th Avenue, Suite 136, New York, NY 10016

Library of Congress Cataloging-in-Publication Data

Names: Lehotsky, Chris, author.
Title: Wizards / Chris Lehotsky.
Description: New York : Cavendish Square Publishing, 2016. |
Series: Creatures of fantasy | Includes index.
Identifiers: LCCN 2016006887 (print) | LCCN 2016007912 (ebook) |
ISBN 9781502618566 (library bound) | ISBN 9781502618573 (ebook)
Subjects: LCSH: Wizards--Juvenile literature.
Classification: LCC BF1611 .L434 2016 (print) | LCC BF1611 (ebook) |
DDC 133.4/3--dc23
LC record available at http://lccn.loc.gov/2016006887

Editorial Director: David McNamara
Editor: Kristen Susienka
Copy Editor: Rebecca Rohan
Art Director: Jeffrey Talbot
Designer: Joseph Macri
Production Assistant: Karol Szymczuk
Photo Research: J8 Media

CONTENTS

INTRODUCTION

Tales of wizards originated in Scotland, Ireland, and Wales. Pictured is a landscape in Scotland.

Since the first humans walked Earth, myths and legends have engaged minds and inspired imaginations. Ancient civilizations used stories to explain phenomena in the world around them, such as the weather, the tides, and natural disasters. As different cultures evolved, so too did their stories. From their traditions and observations emerged creatures with powerful abilities, mythical intrigue, and their own origins. Sometimes, different cultures encouraged various manifestations of the same creature. At other times, these creatures morphed into entirely new beings with greater powers than their predecessors.

Today, societies still celebrate the folklore of their ancestors—on-screen in TV shows and movies such as *Doctor Who, Once Upon a Time,* and *Star Wars,* and in books such as the *Harry Potter* and *Twilight* series. Some of these creatures existed, while others are merely myth.

In the Creatures of Fantasy series, we celebrate captivating stories of the past from all around the world. Each book focuses on creatures both familiar and unknown: the elusive alien, the grumpy troll, the devious demon, the graceful elf, the spellbinding wizard, and the harrowing mummy. Their various incarnations throughout history are brought to life. All have their own origins, their own legends, and their own influences on the imagination today. Each story adds a new perspective to the human experience and encourages people to revisit tales of the past in order to understand their presence in the modern age.

A PRIMER ON WIZARDS

"A wizard is never late, nor is he early.
He arrives precisely when he means to."

GANDALF, *LORD OF THE RINGS: THE FELLOWSHIP OF THE RING*

WIZARDS HAVE FEATURED IN STORIES and mythologies throughout human history. They appear as figures in tall tales, key players in religious historical accounts, subjects of illustrations, and fictional heroes in modern times. Though most people usually think of Merlin from British **Arthurian legend** when they think of wizards, they exist in many other cultures, including China, Japan, and even the Americas. Some wizards possess magical abilities, while others are able to change their shapes. They have enchanted audiences for centuries, and continue to do so in the modern age.

WHAT IS A WIZARD?

The word "wizard" comes from the Middle English *wysard*, meaning "wise one." This word was used in Europe during the

Opposite: A nineteenth-century depiction of a magician.

Middle Ages to describe **philosophers**. They possessed great wisdom and were admired for their knowledge. It was not until the mid-1500s, during the Renaissance, that magic became widely associated with the term. Over the years, figures and tales effectively changed the term "wysard" to "wizard," and the definition evolved to describe a powerful magic-wielding human. So the word has stuck ever since.

Wizards, by today's definition, are people who practice magic. They call upon powers—inaccessible to other people—whether due to innate ability, intense training, or some combination of the two. Throughout history, wizards have been looked on with both fear and wonder.

Most modern people think of wizards as men with long grey beards throwing fireballs and calling on supernatural powers. Perhaps Albus Dumbledore, the wise old headmaster of the Hogwarts School of Witchcraft and Wizardry in J.K. Rowling's Harry Potter series, or Gandalf the Grey from J. R. R. Tolkien's novels *The Lord of the Rings* and *The Hobbit* come to mind. However, throughout the centuries, and most certainly in modern times, wizards can be both men and women. Many stories from the world's civilizations detail great wizards fighting fierce battles using magic, wit, and will. Whether male or female, these abilities can be wielded by anyone with strength, skill, and determination.

Today, the idea of the wizard is perpetuated mostly in literature, popular fantasy books, and film. The various ways authors and screenwriters use and describe wizards continue to fascinate audiences and instill in their minds the perception of the wizard as magical and wise.

A Wizard's Looks

There are many ways to describe a wizard. However, the most popular portrayal seems to be that of an old, bearded man. This image is widely influenced by authors such as J. R. R. Tolkien and older writers of myth and legend.

In writing his epic history of Middle Earth, Tolkien drew on descriptions of wise characters from much older legends and myths. For example, the legend of Merlin and the myths of Odin, the All-Father of Norse mythology, heavily influenced Tolkien's portrayal of Gandalf.

Albus Dumbledore was one of the most well-known wizards in the Harry Potter series.

Another feature associated with wizards was some sort of staff. This walking stick was in some stories an ornately carved object brimming with power. Other times, it was a simple gnarled walking stick meant to help the old man on his journey. As stories of wizards evolved through the centuries, some tales replaced the staff with a magic wand. The wand, like the staff, was an extension of the wizard's will and the object through which he could use his powers to affect reality. Today, stage magicians also use wands, usually with brightly colored tips. The stage magician's wand is an object of misdirection, used to help create illusions and sleight-of-hand tricks.

Wizards in stories take a variety of forms. Some, like Dumbledore, are human but have trained to access magical abilities. Others, like Gandalf, are of a different race entirely. According to Tolkien, Gandalf is a lesser god with great power. He only takes human form to move among the human world. Throughout Tolkien's works, when Gandalf roves amongst mankind, he wears the form of an old man and acts as a mentor figure, usually only taking up arms against other magical beings. His function within

Gandalf the Grey is a helper and a powerful wizard in The Lord of the Rings trilogy.

Tolkien's mythology is to present others with the call to action. He acts as a true leader, helping the people under his care reach their full potential, but rarely actually unveiling his powers.

Not all the wizards in stories and myth are good, however. For every Dumbledore, there is a Voldemort. For every Gandalf, there is a Saruman or a Sauron. In some tales, a wizard who focuses on curses and spell-casting is known as a sorcerer or a dark magician. Instead of building and healing, these antagonists focus on destruction, illness, and death.

Are Wizards Relevant Today?

There is a reason these stories and characters remain so prevalent in films and literature today. By exaggerating people and their abilities to larger-than-life proportions, storytellers can speak to an audience's desire to be greater than they are, to discuss social issues in different contexts, and to entertain, all at the same time.

Today, people are perhaps just as enchanted with the idea of magical humans as people of the Middle Ages were entranced by the lure of a wysard's knowledge. To possess knowledge and magic is to possess power. Films and literature make powerful humans with exceptional abilities come to life. Likewise, magicians keep the spark of enchantment and imagination alive in audiences of old and young alike.

The Druids

Much of our modern understanding of wizards is loosely based on stories about an ancient group of people called Druids. Most writings about these people come from Julius Caesar as well as figures discussed in Irish sagas passed down centuries before him. According to these sources, the Druids were scholars who lived in present-day Ireland, Scotland, and Wales, in the third century BCE. They acted as judges, priests, healers, and historians for their communities. Druids were said to gather in oak forests to sort arguments and make decisions about community life. They had the power to perform sacrifices to improve the health of a community member or to appease the gods whom they worshipped.

Tales of Druids inspired modern images of wizards.

Today, many people relate Druids to wizards, for their mysterious and wise presences in ancient history and folklore. Many illustrations of Druids show them as old, bearded men with flowing robes, gathered in an ancient forest. Many stories of wizards use forest settings as places of solace, thus adapting elements of Druid life to the fictional lives of wizards.

2

WIZARDS THROUGH HISTORY

"Any true wizard, faced with a sign like 'Do not open this door' ... would automatically open the door in order to see what all the fuss is about. This made signs rather a waste of time, but at least it meant that when you handed what was left of the wizard to his grieving relatives you could say, as they grasped the jar, 'We told him not to.'"

TERRY PRATCHETT, *THE LAST CONTINENT*

WIZARDS ARE NOT JUST FICTIONAL characters. Much of their evolution is based on ancient figures from the earliest days of recorded history. Originally, they were simply wise men: seekers of knowledge, prophets, healers, alchemists, and mentors. Over time, elements of magic and sorcery were ascribed to them, making them into the figures we know today. Altogether, the history of wizards is varied and stems across many countries and many eras.

MANY FORMS OF MAGIC

In today's society, the thought of a wizard without magic is difficult to comprehend. Magic as we know it is an essential part

Opposite: A wizard casts a spell.

of a wizard's being. However, in other civilizations and times, magic had a different meaning. The first "wizards" were seekers of knowledge. Thus, knowledge was the first "magic." Many cultures, from Mesopotamia to ancient Egypt, had stories of wise men seeking truth through various means. Sometimes, they studied the stars, patterns of nature, and ways of healing sickness and injury. **Necromancy**, or the ability to speak to and raise the dead, was also popular with many ancient cultures. Over time, stories of seeking truth, knowledge, and explanation for the unknown transformed into exceptional abilities such as controlling weather, healing others, and commanding the dead. All of these elements helped shape the modern perception of wizards.

Wizards in Egypt

One of the most ancient civilizations, Egypt, is also one of the first cultures to influence the history of wizards. Egyptian pharaohs kept trusted aides and advisors as part of their council. Some of these men were purported to be sorcerers with supernatural abilities, such as the power to control the weather and other forces of nature. These men each had a patron god from whom he supposedly derived his powers. Through magical rituals and incantations, they were able to gain superhuman strength and endurance, not only for themselves, but for others as well.

The Bible discusses these Egyptian sorcerers in the Book of Exodus. When Moses appears to channel God's power to attempt to convince the pharaoh to release the imprisoned Hebrew people, the sorcerers are able to replicate every one of Moses's "miracles." However, when faced with an onslaught of plagues, they are defeated. Nevertheless, the pharaoh's

sorcerers were masters of magic and trickery. They held special importance in the court of the kings and helped shape the first perceptions of wizards in society.

Wizards Among the Ancient Greeks

Magic and wizardry are common motifs in the mythology of the ancient Greeks. The very word "magic" stems from the Greek *magoi*. Thus, it is easy to draw a connection between magic and wizardry.

The Greeks had many myths involving humans with special abilities. For example, in the epic poem the *Odyssey*, the title character, Odysseus, battles the Titan Circe, who attacks Odysseus's men with a magic wand. She transforms them into pigs. However, Odysseus is able to shield himself from her attack through the use of a magic herb called moly.

Another major cycle of stories from Greek mythology follows a man named Orpheus. Orpheus is a prophet and a legendary musician, whose music contains magical powers. He has the ability to make even the most violent of predatory animals fall under his control with the enchanting power of his song. The main myth of Orpheus tells of his journey to the underworld, and his attempt to bring his deceased wife, Eurydice, back to the world of the living. Orpheus plays a lyre with magical powers to persuade the god Hades to release Eurydice to him. The power of Orpheus's magic is so strong he succeeds in impressing Hades and convincing him to let Eurydice leave the underworld, as long as Orpheus does not look at her until they are above ground. As the two ascend to the land of the living, Orpheus can't resist looking at his wife, and Eurydice is lost to him forever. However, as the story shows, Orpheus's superhuman abilities were enough to make him persuade even the immortal.

Odin riding his horse Sleipnir.

Norse Mythology and Odin

The Norse people, who lived largely from the ninth to the eleventh centuries in what is now Scandinavia, held a complex religious hierarchy of gods and spirits. The supreme god, Odin, is often represented in stories as a wanderer and a seeker for arcane knowledge who would do anything to gain more power. On one occasion, he is said to have hanged himself, wounded with a spear, from the World Tree. He hung there for nine days without food or water but returned with knowledge of the Nordic Runes, an early writing system. In another story, he gouged out his own eye, exchanging it for "second sight," the ability to see the future. In his wanderer guise, he is described as having a long grey beard, wearing heavy robes, and a large-brimmed hat. Stories of Odin and other mythological magicians, combined with descriptions of the Druids and their practices, contributed to the modern image of a wizard.

Historical Figures

Several real-life people had various powers of wizardry ascribed to them, both in life and then exaggerated upon their deaths. For instance, the famous mathematician Pythagoras was said to have performed many magical acts, including being in two different cities at the same time, predicting several deaths, and being able to control the weather. Empedocles, a poet and scientist who lived a generation after Pythagoras, is credited with the abilities to heal

the sick, raise the dead, and control the weather. He is thought to have been the first philosopher to divide nature and its workings into the four **classical elements**: fire, earth, air, and water.

Zoroaster

Also known as Zarathustra, Zoroaster was an Iranian prophet who lived some time around the year 1500 BCE. He was the founder of the Zoroastrian religion, a monotheistic faith that worships Azhara, meaning "wise lord." Muslims accept Zoroaster as a prophet and Zoroastrianism as an antecedent religion to their own Islamic faith. The Greeks had a different view of Zoroaster as an astrologer and sorcerer. They even credited him with being the inventor of **astrology** and magic itself. Zoroaster's legacy inspired many people, including the Magi in the Old Testament, to follow religions connected to him.

Abe no Seimei

Abe no Seimei was the most well-known wizard figure to come out of the Far East. The exploits attributed to him read almost like a Japanese version of the legend of Merlin. Unlike Merlin, however, his existence is not debated. Abe was a very real person who lived from 921 to 1005 CE. He was advisor to multiple emperors, and at the time he was the greatest teacher of a type of cosmology called *onmyōdō*. Onmyōdō combines the natural sciences (based on the study of the classical elements of earth, wind, water, and fire) with the concept of **yin-yang**, the balance of light and dark or good and evil. He advised the rulers he served specifically from the perspective of onmyōdō. Abe was also a noted diviner and astrologer. Though he was a real person, his attributed magical exploits exist mostly in popular fiction in Japan today.

Faust and
Mephistopheles
playing chess.

Johann Georg Faust

Doctor Faust was an astrologer, alchemist, and magician who lived during the Renaissance period. Soon after his death, his life became the basis for the popular folktale and later, in 1604, a play written by Christopher Marlowe. Both *The Tragical History of the Life and Death of Doctor Faustus* and Johann Wolfgang von Goethe's nineteenth-century epic two-part play *Faust* have become classic examples of the tale.

Little is known with historical accuracy about the real-life Faust. He lived from either around 1480 or 1466 to 1541. From 1506 to the next thirty years, there are records of Faust appearing all over Germany selling his services as a magician, astrologer, alchemist, or physician. There are nearly as many records of him being run out of town accused of being a fraud and a con artist. He was even accused of necromancy on occasion. The last record of Faust before his death was in the city of Münster in 1535 during the Anabaptist rebellion following the Lutheran Reformation.

Johann Faust's legend lived far longer than his sixty or seventy-five years. In both Marlowe's and Goethe's versions of the tale, Faust is a skilled magician but dissatisfied with life. He goes into the forest and summons a demon named Mephistopheles. They make a deal where Faust gains whatever he wants by magical means for the next twenty-four years in exchange for his soul. In Marlowe's telling, Faust repents on the final day of his life, but is too late. Goethe ends the tale on an uplifting note, with Faust's good deeds outweighing the bad, and he gets to go to Heaven rather than Hell.

Ja'far ibn Yahya

Anyone who has seen the animated Disney film *Aladdin* knows the villainous character of the sorcerer and royal vizier, Jafar. He is searching for a magical lamp that holds a genie capable of granting three wishes, that he plans on using to overthrow the kingdom of Agrabah. The famous tale the film is based on, "Aladdin and the Wonderful Lamp," appears in *The Book of One Thousand and One Nights*, sometimes called simply *The Arabian Nights*, depending on translation, as it was originally

Jafar and Iago the parrot in *The Return of Jafar*.

an Arabic source. However, the tale of Aladdin was not originally included in the Arabic book. In fact, the tale, set in China, was added by a French translator, Antoine Galland, and has appeared in most editions of the book since. Though the tale did have an evil sorcerer bent on taking over the kingdom with the aid of a genie, he barely resembled the villain of the film.

Even though the film character of Jafar is very loosely based on an actual person from history, in most of the stories told of Ja'far ibn Yahya, he is the hero. Ja'far lived from 767 to 803 CE and served as vizier to the caliph Harun al-Rashid in Baghdad, Iraq. He is credited as being a proponent of scientific inquiry as well as acquiring the knowledge of papermaking from Chinese prisoners of war.

3

POWERS OF A WIZARD

"A wizard's power of Changing and Summoning can shake the balance of the world. It is dangerous, that power ... It must follow knowledge, and serve need."

Ursula K. Le Guin, *A Wizard of Earthsea*

WIZARDS ARE KNOWN FOR BEING able to tap into various powers that shape the fundamental workings of the world. Typically, these powers revolve around the use of magic. However, other abilities also exist. Most cultures describe these powers in stories. Today, these powers can also be illustrated onscreen, including some of the most prominent abilities assigned to wizards.

HEALING

Healing magic can take on many forms. The most common of these is the use of medicinal herbs. In the past, tribal peoples would rely on a **shaman** or medicine man for a variety of things, from

Opposite: Adriaen van Ostade's painting *An Alchemist*, circa 1661.

weather prediction and control to healing. The shamans would use various herbs ranging from ineffectual plants to actual painkillers. Sometimes, a hallucinogen would be administered, such as a mold or a mushroom. The major difference between this type of healing and going to the doctor and getting a prescription for an antibiotic is the religious aspect. In order for the magic to work, there would usually have to be some sort of sacrifice or prayer to gods/spirits/demons to intercede on the behalf of the practitioner and patient. In stories, magicians and wizards could heal people by touching an injured person. This would transfer power directly from the magician to the patient.

Alchemy

Alchemy is a precursor to modern chemistry in medieval Europe. To many, it was at first considered a type of magic, and the people who practiced it—alchemists—were considered magicians. Alchemists' main goals were focused on trying to change metals, such as copper and lead, into gold and to create a potion, or elixir, that would cure any illness or eliminate any ingested poisons. Many alchemists were also Christians, and it was reasoned that if Jesus could turn water into wine, certainly these men could figure out a way to produce similar feats. They used alchemy to advance science, and some of their "medicines" were disgusting to a modern-day person.

One ingredient in an alchemical cure-all was a bezoar. A bezoar is a mass found in the gastrointestinal tract of many animals that was believed to cure any poison. Often, gallstones from an ox's stomach were used. Other times, the heart and lungs of a viper would be ground together.

Whether alchemists truly worked miracles through their medical practices is debated, but it cannot be ignored that alchemists performed some enchanting experiments.

Prophecy and Divination

Prophecy is a foreknowledge of future events. This knowledge can be a message from a god or divine spirit, or it can simply be a unique inspiration that the prophet interprets to be a **divination**. Every major religion has its prophets, keepers of secret knowledge, and heralds of things to come. Some purported real-life wizards also displayed this power. The Frenchman Michel de Nostredame, or Nostradamus, was one such historical figure. He was a physician who became fascinated by the **occult**. Beginning in 1550, he published annual almanacs. In 1555 he published *Les Propheties*, a book of predictions of future events that is still in print today.

Necromancy

Necromancy is a form of prophecy in a roundabout way. Rather than having knowledge of the future come upon them through divine communication or inspiration, necromancers have to ask for

The Witch of
Endor summons
the ghost of
Samuel with
necromancy.

it. Specifically, necromancy is the art of divination through talking to the dead, whether by summoning their ghosts or by bringing their corpses back to life. There are many rituals surrounding the practices of necromancy, including dressing in the dead person's clothes, wearing various talismans or amulets, and even attempting to conjure demons to borrow their powers. There are multiple stories of necromancy being practiced worldwide in ancient times, including Egypt, Greece, and Rome. Probably the most prominent record of its use comes from the Christian Bible, where Saul had the Witch of Endor raise the spirit of Samuel to provide a prophecy. Necromantic rites can include anything from the use of blood sacrifice to employing a Ouija board to speak to the dead.

Controlling the Elements

Popular stories tell of wizards learning to control the elements, such as water, metal, fire, and earth. Peter S. Beagle's novel *The Last Unicorn*, published in 1968, features the character of Schmendrick, who seeks nothing more than to master spells and become a powerful wizard. His powers eventually lead him to manipulate objects and transform living creatures from one form to another. Other wizards have been depicted as controlling aspects of nature, such as wind, lightning, and rain. In the popular role-playing game *Dungeons and Dragons*, there are two types of wizard, those who control lighting and those who control fire. Each power leads to further traits that can lead the player through the game. Wizards in books such as the Harry Potter series, the Wheel of Time series by Robert Jordan, and *The Name of the Wind* by Patrick Rothfuss also have many characters that try their hand at mastering the powers of weather control and nature manipulation.

Immortality

Some stories have immortal wizards. In *The Last Unicorn*, Schmendrick is immortal until he can become a true wizard. Tolkien's Gandalf, on the other hand, seems to go through stages of immortality. In *The Fellowship of the Ring* he is known as Gandalf the Grey. By the trilogy's end, he has become Gandalf the White. His name is associated with different colors as he reaches different stages of immortality. Immortal wizards make valuable allies and dangerous foes. They have limitless time to master their powers, making it possible for them to keep learning new skills forever; they are always growing, storing, and using their powers.

Naming

A **true name** is a hidden name for a person, place, or thing that encompasses its fundamental nature. A true name is not given or invented by the wizard. Rather, through intensive study and communing with nature, a wizard can intuitively come to know the true name of a thing. True names have great power. When spoken by a wizard, a true name can give the wizard control over it. According to folklore, everything has a unique name. Probably the most common example of true names being used is in the German fairy tale of Rumpelstiltskin. Rumpelstiltskin, a magical creature himself, makes a bargain with a young girl. He agrees to help her spin wool into gold in exchange for her firstborn child. In the end, the main character, now a queen, is able to break this bargain by uttering Rumpelstiltskin's true name. Other examples of wizards using naming in modern literature include *A Wizard of Earthsea* by Ursula K. Le Guin and *The Name of the Wind* by Patrick Rothfuss.

Shamanism

In ancient Asian and indigenous traditions, a shaman is someone who has the ability to enter another state of consciousness, such as a trance, in an effort to interact with the spirit world. They are able to effect **divination** as well as healing while in this altered state. Shamans are generally called to their craft by dreams or other signs from a divinity, though occasionally these powers can be taught and passed on by a mentor. One recurring path to shamanism is that of a person who is sick or wounded, but is then healed and brought back from the brink of death. He or she sees and understands the journey to the spirit world in this way, now having an intimate connection with it. A shaman has various roles, depending on his or her particular culture, but they generally include prophecy, healing, and keeping the traditions of his or her people alive. Originally, shamanism was particularly prevalent in Asia, but examples have been found the world over, from the Americas to Europe. Some of the earliest stories of the wizard Merlin may have evolved from ancient shamanistic practices.

An ancient Egyptian amulet.

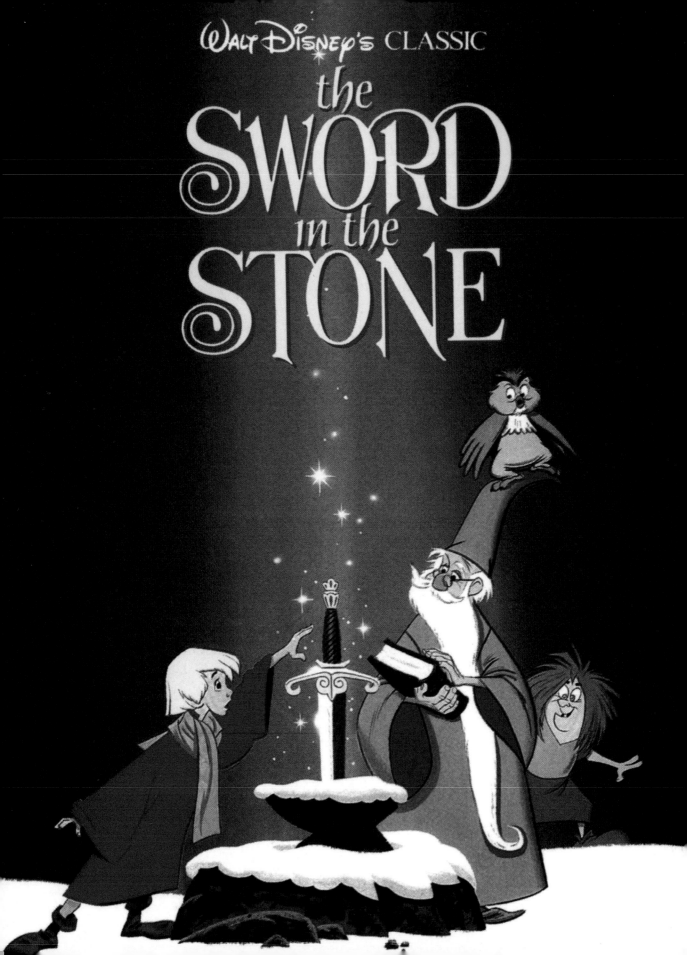

4

THE LEGEND OF MERLIN

"He was one of those people who would be neither a follower nor a leader, but only an aspiring heart, impatient in the failing body which imprisoned it."

T. H. White, *The Sword in the Stone*

MERLIN IS PROBABLY THE MOST ICONIC wizard in all of mythology. His modern resurgence in popularity owes in large part to the character's role in the 1963 Walt Disney film *The Sword in the Stone*. This film was based on a 1938 novel of the same name written by T.H. White, included in his tetralogy collection *The Once and Future King* in 1958. A fifth novel, *The Book of Merlyn*, was published posthumously in 1977. However, all of these works are based on the myths of the legendary King Arthur, which date back to the fifth and sixth centuries.

The Origins of Merlin

Today, Merlin is best known as the wizard and mentor figure who helped raise Arthur Pendragon, later King of Britain. In earlier

Opposite: Artwork for the 1963 film *The Sword in the Stone.*

versions of the story, though, Merlin wasn't a wizard, let alone part of Arthurian legend. In the earliest mention of him, Merlin's name is Myrddin and he lives as a hermit in the woods, driven mad by the horrors of war. In other stories, the exploits of another man, Ambrosius Aurelianus, are attributed to Merlin.

MYRDDIN WYLLT AND AMBROSIUS AURELIANUS

Myrddin Wyllt (Merlin of the Wild) or Merlinus Caledonensis first appeared in six Welsh poems and various stories between 573 and 1136 CE. In the poems, Myrddin was bard and advisor to a Welsh aristocrat named Lord Gwenddoleu. In 573, the lord, along with his army, was killed in the Battle of Arfderydd (now part of southwest Scotland). Myrddin witnessed the slaughter and went mad with grief. He disappeared into the Caledonian Forest and became the Wild Man of the Woods. In some Myrddin stories, he talks with animals and develops the ability of prophecy as a result of his madness. The story of Myrddin, however, is likely taken from an older story from Scotland, centering around a figure named Lailoken. Nevertheless, Myrddin eventually became Merlin, and his story has been told for many centuries all over the world.

The second man contributing to the Merlin history is Ambrosius Aurelianus, the son of a Roman consul who became a military leader against the Saxons in Britain. He lived sometime during the fifth century CE. His life is documented by several historians from the ninth to the eleventh centuries. His exploits were many, and though he didn't win every battle, he led one of the first significant resistances against the invading Saxons. Some of these exploits would later come to be tacked on to Merlin's legend.

Tintagel Castle, in Cornwall, England, is said to be the home of King Arthur.

Geoffrey of Monmouth

While poems and stories about the man had existed prior to the twelfth century, Merlin's history was not written down in length until a bishop and chronicler named Geoffrey of Monmouth wrote the *Historia Regum Britanniae* between 1135 and 1138. This book gave a detailed fictional history of Britain and included many stories of Arthur Pendragon and his father's advisor, Merlin. Many tales found in the work drew on Celtic legends, stories of Myrddin Wyllt, and histories of Ambrosius Aurelianus.

Several events in Merlin's history follow closely with Ambrosius Aurelianus's history. For example, one tale describes the arrival of Ambrosius in Britain. His arrival came at a time when the British King Vortigern was attempting to construct a massive tower, which kept collapsing. Vortigern's advisors, possibly wysards themselves, told him that the only way to complete the building safely was to sprinkle the blood of an orphan child on the ground outside the building's foundation. When Ambrosius, an orphan, was brought before the king, he revealed that the tower kept collapsing because of a battle between two dragons, one red and one white, in a vast underground cavern beneath the structure. He prophesied that the dragons represented the struggle between the Britons and the Saxons, and that the tower would never stand as long as Vortigern led the fight.

Geoffrey used this tale to bring Merlin into his work. Like Ambrosius, Merlin, a fatherless youth, is brought before Vortigern and makes prophesies. Merlin warns Vortigern that Ambrosius, a noble in the *Historia Regum*, and his brother Uther have set sail for war, but he is ignored. In the resulting battle, Vortigern's castle is razed to the ground, and he dies inside. The *Historia Regum* continues to describe the feats of Merlin and Arthur, and the establishment of Arthur's kingdom. It would become one of the most popular works during the Middle Ages and would form the basis of Arthurian legends from the twelfth century onward

Arthurian Legend

Merlin is best presented in the various Arthurian legends contained in the *Historia Regum* as well as others that followed. According to legend, King Arthur was a monarch that united a broken country. He was the son of Uther Pendragon, a king and an enemy of the Saxons.

In *Historia Regum*, Uther Pendragon is aided by Merlin, a wise man and wizard. With his help, Uther Pendragon becomes king and falls in love with a woman named Igerna. Igerna, however, is married to Gorlois, the Duke of Cornwall, and a friend of Uther's. With the help of Merlin's wizardry, Uther sneaks into the duke's palace and conceives Arthur with Igerna. The duke finds out and is killed in the resulting battles. Uther lives and marries Igerna, but soon dies of poisoning. This is the last time Merlin appears in

Geoffrey of Monmouth's telling of the Arthurian story, though it is not the end of Merlin's story.

In the centuries following Monmouth's work, many tales were added to Geoffrey's account of Arthur's rule, both in English and in French. Some of these are stories of the Knights of the Round Table and the quest for the Holy Grail, while others are of Merlin and his continued involvement with the Pendragon kings.

Over time, stories of Merlin's help in raising and advising young Arthur Pendragon were written and became part of Merlin's current history.

Le Morte d'Arthur

Le Morte d'Arthur, which is French for "the death of Arthur," is the basis for all future retellings of Arthurian legend. Authored by Sir Thomas Malory and published in 1485, the story takes all of the known stories of Arthur, Merlin, and the Knights of the Round Table and weaves them into an epic tragedy.

In the tales, when Arthur is a newborn, he is taken to and raised in the home of a country lord, and so is unknown to the court when Uther dies without an heir. The country is in turmoil over who will become the new king. Merlin, who influences Arthur's life at many stages, has placed a sword through an anvil on top of a large rock near the town where Arthur grows up. The sword is engraved with the words:

King Arthur asks the Lady of the Lake for the sword Excalibur.

"Whoso pulleth out this sword from this stone is right wise King born of all England." However, nobody can pull it out, until Arthur comes along. Though the circumstances that bring him to pulling the sword out differ from one story to the next, when Arthur does so, he is proclaimed king and is immediately joined by Merlin, his father's advisor. He soon consolidates the kingdom, establishes the Knights of the Round Table, and brings peace to the region for a time. However, there eventually surfaces a prophecy that the king will die of patricide. Merlin advises the king to take care of the matter. Though to his knowledge he has had no children, Arthur takes Merlin's advice and commands that all young boys of a certain age be gathered and sent away on a boat. The boat is lost at sea in a storm, and all aboard are killed, except for Arthur's bastard son Mordred, who will grow up to fulfill the prophecy despite Merlin's attempt to intervene.

In this work, more is added to Merlin's story. He plays a key role of advisor to Arthur and gains a reputation as a strong and powerful commander of magic. He even falls in love. Nimue, the Lady of the Lake, eventually enters the story and gives to Arthur the legendary sword Excalibur. On meeting her, Merlin falls madly in love, but Nimue does not reciprocate his feelings. Finally, she tells him that she will never love him unless he teaches her all of his magic and they become equals. Though he can see the future, Merlin sees no other way forward than to teach her. Hoping to change his visions of what is to come, he instructs her in the ways of his powers. Eventually, after he has taught her everything, Nimue bounds Merlin inside a tomb of stone, where he dies.

The Once and Future King

While Malory's *Le Morte d'Arthur* is the first English-language version of Arthur's legend, it is nearly unreadable today, as it was written in an English dialect called Middle English. In 1938, T.H. White published *The Sword in the Stone*, a work based on Malory's English tale. White's stories reframed the Arthurian legend even further, focusing primarily on Arthur's childhood (barely dealt with at all by Malory) and teachings by Merlin, a wizard who perceives time backwards, thus knowing the future.

In this version of the story, which is set sometime during the thirteenth century, Merlin plays a large role in Arthur's education. At times, Merlin will turn Arthur into various animals in order to teach a specific lesson. Most of these lessons center around changing Arthur's political mind. The prevalent philosophy during the time period the story is set in was that "Might makes right." Merlin instead advocates a philosophy of chivalry, focusing on protecting the weak and providing for justice in the kingdom of Camelot.

Other stories have since expanded the Arthurian tale and Merlin's role. Marion Zimmer Bradley explored Merlin as a teacher and role model to the young king in her retelling of the Arthurian legend called *The Mists of Avalon*. T. A. Barron imagined Merlin's youth in the young adult fantasy novel *The Lost Years of Merlin*. The wizard continues to be popular in modern times, especially in books and TV adaptations, fascinating audiences of all ages.

Above: Stonehenge as viewed from the north.

Stonehenge

According to the *Historia Regum Britanniae*, Merlin was also helpful in creating Stonehenge, a giant stone burial monument in Wiltshire, England. The stones used in the construction of the monument are said to be healing rocks, brought across the ocean from Africa by giants. They built the ring of stones much as it stands today, but on Mount Killaraus in Ireland. According to Monmouth, following a great battle in the fifth century, Aurelius Ambrosius, ruler of Britain, wants to build a monument to three thousand fallen nobles slain in a battle against the Saxons. He sends Uther Pendragon, along with the wizard Merlin and fifteen thousand knights, to tear down Stonehenge and carry it back across the sea to be rebuilt near Salisbury, where the

fallen nobles were buried. All attempts to move the stones by hand fail miserably, though, until Merlin, with "gear and skill," disassembles the monument and sends it back to England to be rebuilt and dedicated in honor of the fallen.

In actuality, this story is rooted in folklore. Modern radiocarbon dating technology has led archaeologists to believe that the earliest phases of the construction of the monument and the circular earthen bank and ditch that surround it were completed around 3100 BCE, with the giant bluestone dolmens being placed between 2400 and 2200 BCE. However, not all is fiction. Archaeologists have discovered that Stonehenge may have originally been a burial ground, having found human remains dating from 3000 to 2500 BCE. The site is on the UNESCO list of World Heritage Sites, sharing a listing with nearby Avebury Henge.

SOCIETAL REACTIONS TO WIZARDRY

"If any wizard therefore or person imbued with magical contamination who is called by custom of the people a magician ... should be apprehended in my retinue, or in that of the Caesar, he shall not escape punishment and torture by the protection of his rank."

CODEX THEODOSIANUS

WIZARDS AND OTHER PEOPLE WHO are said to practice magic have occupied myriad roles in civilization through the ages. They have been fictional characters of wisdom, sources of evil, and even real-life victims of persecution. Magic itself has endured ridicule, speculation, and contempt throughout the centuries. It has a varied and interesting history, as do the people who are said to wield it. Society's perception of both has changed throughout the generations.

The Ancient Mediterranean World

In ancient Greek mythology, for the most part, magic and sorcery were looked on in a positive light, such as Orpheus's healing songs

Opposite: Frans II the Younger Francken's An Incantation Scene, circa 1606.

and the uses of rare herbs with "magical" healing properties. By the third century BCE, stories of wizards or sorcerers with unlimited power were rare, but the Greek people accepted healers and prophets as regular and normal parts of society. To some degree, magic and belief in the supernatural was a large part of society. Many people of the time believed in and accepted the arts of alchemy. They considered alchemists more or less scientists. However, protective charms and amulets were commonly available. The more superstitious people wore them to protect them from any curse that might be cast upon them. It was also common to seek out a healer to help treat medical conditions or injuries.

The Roman Empire had a less forgiving attitude toward the employment of magical arts. Though alchemy and astrology were thought of as sciences, people accused of practicing magic were perceived as threats and were persecuted. Various codes of law, such as the *Codex Theodosianus*, prohibited the practices of witchcraft and wizardry.

The Middle Ages

With the rise of Christianity in Eastern Europe in the fifth century CE and the fall of the Roman Empire, a widespread suppression of magic began. The official view of the Catholic Church was that magic wielders were consorting with powers not of the one true God, which therefore made them enemies of God. According to the books of Deuteronomy and Exodus, Hebrew law specifically prohibits witchcraft (synonymous with wizardry in translation). Though the Catholic Church itself did not conduct witch trials, there were laws against the practices of magic. By the time Charlemagne ruled the Holy Roman Empire in

the ninth century, belief in witchcraft was outlawed and seen as superstitious and heretical.

The Catholic Inquisitions were instituted beginning in the twelfth century in France. Originally meant to combat the heresies the Catholic Church saw in the Lutheran Reformation, these offices were eventually expanded to specifically include witch-hunts in 1326. By this point in time, witchcraft had become synonymous with devil worship in the eyes of many.

This painting shows a witch convicted by the Inquisition.

The Renaissance

By the 1400s and 1500s, magic as a science was becoming popular again. Once more, the learned thinkers in society were dabbling in magical arts such as healing, incantation, and divination. In order to evade persecution by the ongoing Inquisitions, however, authors took great care to speak against malicious and black magic, such as necromancy. In this way, they could stay on the Catholic Church's good side and avoid execution.

In an attempt to explain the natural world with magic, some people looked to stories of the Celtic Druids, exaggerated through retellings from wise men into skilled magicians. Because very little was written down before the Romans conquered Europe, these studies were a frustrating dead end due to sheer lack of information. Though there was an interest in the occult and divination of the future, other men like Leonardo da Vinci were trying to describe

A portrait of Sir Isaac Newton.

natural phenomena that there were no words or theories for. Magic was a good jumping-off point for this. Though discovery of **lift and drag forces** was centuries away, da Vinci's notebooks contained drawings of a flying machine, hundreds of years before the invention of the airplane. Even Isaac Newton, in the late seventeenth century, was versed in the studies of alchemy. Indeed, man's attempts to try to understand nature by magical means eventually led to his understanding of the world by scientific and mathematical implementations.

Though accusations of malicious wizardry and witchcraft were never common, in 1692 over fifty people were arrested in a bout of mass hysteria that swept Salem, Massachusetts, and several neighboring towns. Nineteen people were convicted and executed before the year was over and the populace came to their senses.

Modern Times

Following the mass hysteria of the witch-hunts in the United States, humanity entered an age of scientific and industrial revolution. From the eighteenth century onward, some of the most unexplainable mysteries became mundane as scientists discovered explanations and theories behind the underlying laws of nature. Not only that, but the average person's quality of life dramatically improved. Life expectancies increased. As fewer people needed to resort to mysticism and wizardry, the persecution of the practitioners waned also.

Today, there are still people who believe in and practice mysticism. Such groups include the religion of Wicca and the Hermetic Order of the Golden Dawn. These groups saw a large increase in membership in the 1960s and 1970s with the hippie and counterculture movements, as a reaction against the many conflicts associated with the Cold War between the United States and the Soviet Union. Because there is less magic and more technology in the everyday world, the majority of society realizes that these groups pose little to no threat to the order of civilization.

The Price of Power

In nearly all magical traditions and literature, using magic comes with a cost. A wizard's power is limited. Some wizards gain their power from a god by praying or making a sacrifice. These sacrifices can be anything from burning something valuable, such as grain or meat, to giving up a month or year of their life, or even to killing something or someone with the express purpose of using their life energies to power the magic. The ancient Celtic Druids were said to have burned people alive in a giant wooden cage known today as a wicker man. Stories of this have even made their way into modern cinema with the 1973 film *The Wicker Man* and the 2006 remake of the same name.

A wicker man.

Some other wizards pull their powers from an infinite pool of power, such as the True Source that drives the Wheel of Time in the book series by Robert Jordan. In a case like this, the price of using the magic is likely to be in mental exertion and extreme concentration. An added cost is that the use and mastery of this type of magic is likely to involve extensive training over the course of many years. Every tradition is different, but magical powers nearly always come with a cost.

SHAPESHIFTING WIZARDS

"At this hour
Lie at my mercy all mine enemies."
WILLIAM SHAKESPEARE, *THE TEMPEST*

SHAPESHIFTERS, OR SKIN-CHANGERS, appear in many different cultures, from the werewolves of Europe to the Rakshasa (demons that can take human form) and Naga (snakes that can transform into humans) of India. In the British Isles, wizards are often portrayed with the ability to shapeshift. Sometimes they transform into animals, other times into various human forms. However, other cultures have wizard-like characters that also change their shapes at will.

The Navajo Skin-Walker

The Native American Navajo fear a type of wizard they call *yee naaldlooshii*, which translates as "with it, he goes on all fours." The yee naaldlooshii is also known as a skin-walker.

Opposite: A wolf clan chief in British Columbia, Canada. Some Native American warriors wore animal skins to represent their clan and to channel the animal's power.

Skin-walkers are male practitioners of the Navajo "Witchery Way." They are wizards with the power to wear the form of an animal. Indeed, for those skin-walkers who have the ability to transform into different animals, these choices are important, as the transformation comes with all of the strengths and weaknesses that animal may have. It is even believed by some that a skin-walker can take the face of another human being. If a person makes eye contact with one, the wizard can project himself into that person's body, becoming him or her to all outside appearances. Other Navajo believe that eye contact only lets the skin-walker feed off of one's energy. Stories of the yee naaldlooshii are scattered and rarely written down for fear of retribution, as a skin-walker wizard's primary motivation is revenge. They are cold and calculating, changing forms at will to serve their ends.

In the stories that are told about skin-walkers, the most common way to start down the path to becoming one is to commit murder, generally that of a close immediate family member. Other times it could just be a person the would-be wizard wants to imitate or become. Typically, these wizards are described as wearing animal skins, particularly the skins of the animals they can change into. For this reason, very few animal pelts are worn ceremonially among the Navajo, as the wearing of such is a giveaway of being a skin-walker.

Though they can't cross the threshold of a home without invitation, the skin-walkers can imitate the voices of other people, or even a child's cry, in an attempt to entice someone out of doors at night. These wizards are also known to create various charms and amulets, to assist them in gaining the power of fear and control over the people they attack. These charms can be made out of anything owned by the person they are attacking. Skin-walkers

sometimes use more violent aids as well. These wizards make a magical powder called corpse dust from the ground-up bones of children. They blow this dust in the faces of their victims, causing their tongues and throats to swell up and turn black. The victim convulses and dies.

Some Navajo have tried to shoot skin-walkers, but rarely are they killed or even wounded. Generally, the wizard will lead their pursuer on a merry chase while in animal form, sometimes ending at the home of a trusted friend or family member in an effort to sow discord. If a person learns the identity of a skin-walker, he can speak the wizard's true name, and all of the wrongs he has committed will reflect back on him, causing sickness and death in a matter of days.

Shapeshifting Wizards of Mesoamerica

The **Nagual**, or Nahual, is a **shapeshifting** wizard very similar to the Navajo yee naaldlooshii that lives in Central America. Legends of the Nagual wizards date back to the times before Christopher Columbus arrived in the New World and brought European influences to the Americas. Naguals can transform into local animals such as the jaguar or puma. These shapeshifting wizards can only change into one type of animal. The biggest difference between the Navajo skin-walker and the Nagual is that the Nagual is not inherently evil. Depending on the personality of the Nagual, his powers can be used for either good or ill. The powers of these wizards are not obtained through malicious rites; rather, they are related to the practitioner's birthdate on the Mesoamerican calendar. Certain dates correspond to a stronger affinity with certain animals. Not only does the date determine if a person is born a Nagual, but it also determines the singular animal that person can transform into, whether it is a bird, a land animal, or even rarely, an aquatic creature. The powers of the Nagual have even been associated with a patron deity in the Aztec religion, the god Tezcatlipoca.

Shapeshifting Wizards in Fiction

Shapeshifting wizards appear throughout modern popular fantasy fiction as well. Younger wizards in J.K. Rowling's Harry Potter series transform into both animal and other human forms through use of a special potion called polyjuice, while experienced wizards such as Professor McGonagall and the Marauders learn how to transform into animal form at will. Beings called the *Valar* and *Maiar* (including Gandalf) in Tolkien's *The Silmarillion* can also change their forms willingly. In *The Hobbit*, Bilbo and his company encounter a skin-changer named Beorn, who can change into an enormous black bear, and who later assists them in the Battle of the Five Armies.

Throughout the Arthurian legends are accounts of Merlin using his powers to shapeshift. In one story, he disguises himself as a woodcutter, a burly man with a big bristly beard and a giant axe on his shoulder. In another story, he appears as a peasant boy shepherding a flock. Through use of his magical abilities, Merlin is a master of disguise, but his powers are not limited to changing only his own appearance. In the tale of Uther and Igerna, Merlin uses his magic to transform Uther, disguising him so he can enter the house of Gorlois and pursue his forbidden love.

Most famously, however, in T. H. White's *The Sword in the Stone*, Merlin uses his shapeshifting powers to transform the young Arthur into various animal forms as part of his political and philosophical teachings. In his first lesson, Merlin turns Arthur into a fish to

teach him about the monarchy of the fishes in the moat. In another, Arthur is transformed into a bird and spends a night amongst the other birds living in a militant society in the rafters. In a third adventure, Merlin changes Arthur into an ant to learn about the authoritarian society of the ants. In yet more lessons, Arthur is transformed into a goose and later into a badger. It is shortly after these final lessons that Arthur pulls the sword from the stone and is proclaimed king of England.

The Sorcerer's Apprentice

One of the most iconic uses of shapeshifting in modern film is also one of the oldest, appearing in the 1940 Walt Disney film, *Fantasia*. *Fantasia* is a film with no dialogue. Instead it uses a sequence of animated short episodes set to famous pieces of classical music. "The Sorcerer's Apprentice," a piece by French composer Paul Dukas, is based on a poem of the same name, written by Johann Goethe. In Disney's animation, Mickey Mouse is the apprentice to a great sorcerer, Yen Sid. He is assigned chores to do. After fetching several buckets of water, Mickey tries to simplify things through use of magic. He animates a broom, bringing it to life, and changes its shape, giving it a semblance of arms and legs. The broom proceeds to carry buckets of water as Mickey happily dozes off, dreaming of being a powerful wizard. He wakes up to discover the room rapidly filling with water. He takes an axe, chopping the broom to splinters, but the animation spell remains. The splinters of broom grow arms and legs and begin carrying water buckets again, flooding the wizard's workshop completely. Finally, the sorcerer returns, banishing the water with a gesture, and removes the magic from the broom. Breathing a sigh of relief, his apprentice resumes his chores, realizing that he still has much to learn.

The sorcerer's apprentice directing his brooms in *Fantasia*, 1940.

BELL
OUT OF ORDER
PLEASE KNOCK

TODAY'S WIZARDING WORLD

"In dreams, we enter a world that is entirely our own."

ALBUS DUMBLEDORE, *HARRY POTTER AND THE PRISONER OF AZKABAN*

WHILE WIZARDS AND THEIR MAGICAL powers have long been part of tradition and folklore, and in some cases believed to be real, science and technology have put to rest many superstitions in modern civilization. That is not to say that there is no place for wizards in today's world. On the contrary, the stories of wizards will always captivate humanity, and the idea of magic will continue to enthrall and entrance.

WIZARDS IN MODERN LITERATURE

Some of the most iconic wizards have featured in literary and popular fiction books. Some of the most successful are

Opposite: This scene from The Wizard of Oz shows Dorothy and her friends waiting to meet the Wizard.

The Wonderful Wizard of Oz by L. Frank Baum in 1900, *The Hobbit* by J. R. R. Tolkien in 1937, *The Eye of the World* by Robert Jordan in 1990, and the Harry Potter series by J.K. Rowling, which started in 1997.

The Wonderful Wizard of Oz tells of the adventures of Dorothy, a young girl from Kansas, who is transported to the land of Oz, and her quest to return home. Oz's population includes many magical creatures, including both good and evil witches, but ultimately, the Wizard is the one in charge. By the tale's end it is discovered the Wizard is a normal man without magical powers. Despite this, Dorothy succeeds in defeating the Wicked Witch of the West and returning home to Kansas. A successful children's book, the original story spawned thirteen sequels as well as a 1939 feature film.

The Hobbit tells the story of unlikely events, at least partially orchestrated by the wizard Gandalf the Grey, which happen to the hobbit Bilbo Baggins. Published in 1937, the book was so well received that Tolkien's publisher requested a sequel. Originally meant as another children's book like *The Hobbit*, *The Lord of the Rings* became a deeply involved story that drew heavily upon his invented language and mythology. It furthers the stories of Gandalf and Bilbo and introduces plenty of new wizards and other magical beings in a conflict of epic proportions. For economic reasons, it was published in three volumes across 1954 and 1955. It was a runaway success and is still in print today in multiple editions. Following his father's

death, Christopher Tolkien published *The Silmarillion*, based on his father's notes, in 1977. In addition to providing a massive amount of backstory, *The Silmarillion* provided an origin story for the popular wizards of Tolkien's world.

The popularity of wizards in fiction would slowly diminish through the 1980s, then see a dramatic shift in January 1990 with the publication of Robert Jordan's *The Eye of the World*, the first volume in what would grow to be a fifteen-volume series called The Wheel of Time. Though not as universally loved as Tolkien's books, this epic tale made it possible for other stories to be told by proving the possibility of commercial success for a giant multivolume fantasy series.

J.K. Rowling's *Harry Potter and the Philosopher's Stone* was released in 1997 to an appreciative young adult audience. The titular character learns about his heritage as the son of two wizards who were killed by an evil sorcerer who, though defeated, threatens to return. This novel, where all of the main characters are attending a school specifically to learn to be wizards, eventually spawned six sequels to Harry's story as well as other books about the same world.

WIZARDS REIMAGINED

Wizards aren't only restricted to traditional fantasy trappings. One of the most popular modern-day imaginings of the wizard could be argued to be the Jedi of George Lucas's Star Wars universe. Jedi such as Obi-Wan Kenobi are warrior monks and keepers of

Sir Alec Guinness as the Jedi Knight Obi-Wan Kenobi in *Star Wars: Episode IV – A New Hope*, 1977.

the peace. A combination of knight and wizard, they do battle with lightsabers (sword-like objects) and follow a chivalrous code. They also have access to a great and unseen power. Jedi are great leaders, who only resort to combat when words fail. Obi-Wan even dresses like a traditional wizard with a heavy cloak and a grey beard. Through meditation, the Jedi can sense the Force, an energy field that surrounds and binds all matter together. After much training, a Jedi can begin to influence the world around him or her by manipulating the Force.

The concept of the Jedi as wizard draws on other cultural influences as well. The Jedi and their counterparts, the Sith, hold ideas largely derived from a philosophies from ancient China called Taoism and yin-yang. Taoism, meaning "the way" or "the path," focuses on people living in harmony with one another. The light and dark sides of the Force draw on concepts of yin-yang. The Jedi are so popular with audiences that there have been seven *Star Wars* films released to date, with many more anticipated.

WIZARDS ON FILM AND IN REALITY

Though there have been many films starring wizard characters over the years, at the end of the twentieth century, technology had finally advanced far enough to create spectacular special effects showing wizardry. By the time *Harry Potter and the Goblet of Fire*, the fourth book in the series, was released in 2000, a film adaptation of the first book was set to release alongside an adaptation of the first volume of *The Lord of the Rings* the following year. Both were hits

The popular Harry Potter series has inspired a theme park featuring Hogwarts castle.

at the box office and ensured the longevity of fantasy and stories about wizards for years to come. To date, there are eight *Harry Potter* films and six films based on Tolkien's works.

In 2010, the *Harry Potter*–themed Wizarding World of Harry Potter opened as part of the Islands of Adventure park at the Universal Orlando Resort in Orlando, Florida. It includes several attractions within a recreation of the Hogwarts castle as seen in the films. In 2014, Universal Studios opened its own Wizarding World, featuring a recreation of Diagon Alley, the magical shopping district of London described in the books, as well as several other unique rides and attractions. A similar park opened at Universal Studios Japan that same year. A fourth *Harry Potter*–themed attraction opened at Universal Studios Hollywood in 2016.

Wizards on the Small Screen

Wizards are not only limited to the movie theaters nowadays. More and more fantasy-themed television shows and miniseries are being made every year. A Merlin miniseries starring Martin Short aired on NBC in 1998. In Great Britain, a Merlin television show ran for sixty-five episodes on the BBC. Terry Goodkind's *Sword of Truth* novels were adapted for television as *Legend of the Seeker* in 2008. In 2016, MTV began a television series based on Terry Brooks's *Shannara Chronicles*. An adaptation of Patrick Rothfuss's *The Name of the Wind* is in development by Lionsgate as of early 2016. All of these feature prominent characters with the powers of wizardry.

WIZARDS OF THE MODERN AGE

It is highly unlikely that the likes of Gandalf and Dumbledore will be seen in real life, throwing fireballs across New York City streets. However, the spirit of wizardry still exists in the form of stage magicians. Modern magicians generate a variety of effects, primarily through use of misdirection, for public entertainment. Types of stage magic can include card tricks, making an object appear or disappear, making an object or person appear to levitate, or escaping from dangerous mechanisms. Though these are tricks and not a showing of an otherworldly power, these modern magicians are the successors of wizardry on the stage. Famous modern stage magicians include David Copperfield, Siegfried and Roy, Penn and Teller, and David Blaine.

Glossary

alchemy A pseudo-scientific process by which practitioners attempted to convert base metals into gold and to create a magical elixir that would cure any ailment.

Arthurian legend Any story in the British folklore and mythology surrounding King Arthur.

astrology A form of divination involving the study of the movements of the planets and the stars and the process of using that to draw up horoscopes in an attempt to predict the future.

classical elements The four classical elements of natural philosophy are earth, fire, air, and water.

divination Prophets seek knowledge of the future by the magical art of divination, which can take many forms.

lift and drag forces The forces that act on the wings of a bird or an airplane to keep it aloft.

Nagual A shapeshifting wizard from Central America.

necromancy The black magical art of bringing the dead back to life, or summoning their ghosts, to gain knowledge from them.

occult Knowledge of the paranormal.

onmyōdō An ancient Japanese philosophy that combines the study of the classical elements with the philosophy of the yin-yang.

philosopher A person who searches for wisdom and knowledge.

shaman A person who, by entering an altered state of consciousness, can communicate with and interact with the spirit world to gain knowledge or effect healing.

shapeshifting The magical art of transforming into an animal or other human form.

true name A secret, hidden name that represents the full nature of a specific object or being. True names have magical power if used by one with the knowledge.

yee naaldlooshii A shapeshifting wizard, the Navajo skin-walker.

yin-yang A Chinese representation of the balance of light and dark, or good and evil.

To Learn More About Wizards

Books

Denzel, Jason. *Mystic*. New York: Tor Books, 2015.

Rothfuss, Patrick. *The Name of the Wind*. New York: DAW , 2007.

Sanderson, Brandon. *Steelheart*. New York: Delacorte Press, 2013.

Website

Pottermore

www.pottermore.com
The official website of Harry Potter author J. K. Rowling for new content pertaining
to the world of the Harry Potter series.

Film

The Lord of the Rings: The Fellowship of the Ring. Directed by Peter Jackson. New Line
Cinema, 2001. DVD.

Bibliography

Goss, K. David. *The Salem Witch Trials: A Reference Guide*. Westport, CT: Greenwood Press, 2008. Ebook edition.

Homer. *The Odyssey*. Translated by E.V. Rieu. Harmondsworth, UK: Penguin, 1945.

Jordan, Robert. *The Eye of the World*. New York: Tor Books, 1990.

Kluckhohn, Clyde, and Dorothea Leighton. *The Navaho*. Cambridge, UK: Harvard University Press, 1974.

Malory, Sir Thomas. *Le Morte d'Arthur*. Public Domain: 1471. Ebook edition.

Rowling, J. K. *Harry Potter and the Sorcerer's Stone*. New York: Scholastic, 1999.

Ruickbie, Leo. *Faustus: The Life and Times of a Renaissance Magician*. Stroud, UK: History Press, 2009.

Tolkien, J. R. R. *The Lord of the Rings*. Boston, MA: Houghton Mifflin, 1987.

Vitebsky, Piers. *Shamanism*. Norman, OK: University of Oklahoma Press, 2001.

White, T. H. *The Once and Future King*. New York: Ace, 1987.

Index

Page numbers in **boldface** are illustrations. Entries in **boldface** are glossary terms.

About the Author

Chris Lehotsky has worked as a musician, in construction, retail management, and band instrument repair. He loves to travel, and has visited all of the lower forty-eight states by car. He lives in western New York.